I Had to Prove Myself

Myself

EILEEN DISTASIO-CLARK

With Great Love and Appreciation to Those Who Have and Do Bless My Life

My Family:

Joseph DeStasio Sr. & Miriam Lucille Baragone DeStasio, My Late Parents.

Andrea Jean DeStasio McIntosh, My Older Sister and Their Families.

Joseph DeStasio Jr., My Younger and Only Brother and Their Families.

Donna Marie DeStasio Wagner, My Younger Sister and Their Families.

My Children:

Eileen, Rebekah, Rachel, S. Michael,

Jennifer, Sharon, Tara, Stephanie,

Apryll, Mikaelah, & M. Trevor

and THEIR Families!!

ACKNOWLEDGEMENTS

First and foremost, I express, deeply, my sincere gratitude to our Heavenly Father for blessing me with the gift and talent of writing! I know I could not do what I do without His assistance.

I also want to acknowledge and express gratitude to the members of my birth family—Joseph Sr., Miriam, Andrea, Joseph Junior, and Donna. All the experiences of my childhood years, experiences that taught me so very much and enabled me to reveal my true self to myself, came about through my experiences and relationships with them.

And, of course, it goes without saying, but I will say it anyway: I also want to acknowledge and note my gratitude to my children, Eileen, Rebekah, Rachel, S. Michael, Jennifer, Sharon, Tara, Stephanie, Apryll, Mikaelah, and M. Trevor, and their families! Through multiple things they said to me, over multiple years, I finally came to the realization that

Heavenly Father gave me the gift of writing and opened the doors to these experiences because He knew that by sharing them with others, others could feel His love too.

And He definitely wants us all to know that He, Heavenly Father, Heavenly Mother, and Jehovah truly do loves us!!!

INTRODUCTION

There are sixteen books in this series, which I refer to as, *"The Ellie Series."* All of the characters in these stories portray real people from my life. The main characters depict the members of my family: Daddy is my daddy; Mommy is my mommy; Jeannie is my older sister; Junior is my brother; Maria is my younger sister, and Ellie is me. Now, those are not our actual first names, but they do reference us.

The first story in the series presents our Heavenly Father's Plan of Salvation and takes place in the Pre-Earth World. Now, of course, because we all—when we were born—received what is known as The Veil of Forgetfulness, I do not actually remember everything from or about the Pre-Earth World, but I do know about and understand it from much study and worship as a member of The Church of Jesus Christ of Latter-Day Saints, and memories restored to me through the Holy Spirit. So, from this story there is much truth to be learned.

The last story in the series is set in the Post-Mortal World, and presents a depiction of what happens to us after this life. Again, because I have not gone there yet, I cannot say I 'remember' this. But I have also learned about the Post-Mortal World from much study and worship as a member of The Church of Jesus Christ of Latter-Day Saints.

All of the other stories are based on true events from my life; events that actually occurred when and how they are depicted in these stories. I chose these events because they are among the many occurrences in my life that presented—or revealed that which I already knew without having to be taught—Principles of Eternal Truths.

Also, I chose these events as the settings for my stories because they depict wonderful learning moments from my childhood and adolescent years, lessons that have blessed and benefited me throughout the whole of my life and will forever continue to do so. Also, through these great truths and their consequences in my life, I have been able to share them with many others, whose lives have also been blessed by them.

So, please read and enjoy, then care and share the messages and stories with others!!

Now, there are also a couple of things you can look for:

In each story, the title of the previous story is presented in *italicized* form, the title of the next story is presented in *Capitalized Italicized* form, and the title of the story being read is presented in **emboldened** form.

Also, every story has at least one word that is uncommon or 'created.'

So, as you read, search, find, and have fun!

I HAD TO PROVE MYSELF

It was a pretty nice, comfortably cold, clear, crisp February day. The sun was actually shining, though that was not something too typical for a mid-winter, Pennsylvania late afternoon, but shining it was, and Ellie liked that! It made her feel good! And that was something she really needed, as she walked home from school that day.

Now, think not that it had been a bad day at school, because it had not been. Nope! Not bad at all. School had been as good as it usually was for Ellie. Remember? Ellie loved school, and that day had been an even better-than-usual day! Her teachers were all in good moods, so no one got in trouble for anything, even though some of the boys in some of her classes did *Some Pretty Crazy Things*, and some of the girls in some of her other classes gave some pretty ridiculous answers to some of the questions their teachers had asked. But, overall, it had been a pretty good day, until basketball practice.

Side Note:** Because Ellie was so small, no one ever wanted her on their team for any kind of game or sport. No matter how good she actually was, at least at some of the games they played, everyone was so sure that she would be the reason they lost—if they let her play—that no one ever wanted her to play. And, sad but true, even the coaches of the girls' hockey and basketball teams seemed to feel that way too. So, needless to say, but I am saying anyway, practices were usually less than joyful, and that day was no different! Now, back to the other side.

It really did not take Ellie long to get home, after all, she only lived about three blocks from the high school, but when she got home, she did not go into the house. Instead, she went into the yard. Now, you may be thinking that you know why she went into the yard. You probably think she went into the yard to sit under the Catalpa tree, but you would be wrong. Well, okay, I guess you would be right, but you would be wrong too because, while she did go into the yard to go to the Catalpa tree, she did not go to sit under it; she went to sit IN it!

Yes, you read that correctly, and it should be no surprise. You must know by now that Ellie always liked to climb the Catalpa, trying to get to the highest branches where she was sure the angels always sat. And that day, she really, really, rea... well, you know what I mean; she really needed to talk to them.

So, after brushing all the snow out of the little red wagon that was under Catalpa and putting her school bag in it, she stepped onto the big rock that was just under the lowest branch, jumped up, grabbed hold of the branch, pulled herself up onto the branch, and began climbing, until she made her way up to a big branch, a really big branch, about halfway between the bottom of Catalpa's twisty trunk and the tips of the highest branches, which as always were swaying back and forth, and forth and back, and back and fo… well, you know what I am saying. I know you must know because I know I have said it many times before. Anyway, it was on that branch, after brushing the snow off of it, that she sat quietly, leaning back against Catalpa's twisty trunk and looking up at those swaying branches, that she told *the angels in their backyard tree* all about how she was feeling, and why, and this is what she told them.

"I guess I am just not good enough for anything," she began, with tears welling up in her eyes. "Everybody seems to think that I will mess things up just because I am too small, and I talk too softly, and I write too tiny, and I am too nice… which is silly. How could anyone be too nice? Anyway, no one seems to think I can do anything, especially when it comes to games and sports. No matter what they are playing, nobody ever wants me to play with them. Even when I have shown them that I can do pretty good at lots of things, they always seem to think I will be good at nothing."

Ellie paused for a moment, wiped away the tears that were now running down her cheeks, sighed, and then, looking back up at the swaying branches, and started talking to the angels again, she continued with, "But it is not just games and sports, and it is not just the other kids, either; it is teachers too. Remember Mrs. Shoder, my sixth-grade teacher? Well, even though I got good grades, really good grades, in everything, and she knew that I already knew that I wanted to go to college, she would not assign me to the A Section."

Another **Side Note:** When Ellie went to school, high schools, at least the ones where Ellie lived, had two sections: the A or Academic Section for the kids who were planning to go to college after graduating from high school, and the B or Business Section for kids who were not planning to go to college after high school. Which section a student was assigned, by their sixth-grade teacher usually was, and was always supposed to be, determined by their preference AND their grades, not just by their preference, nor just by their grades, and definitely not just by the teacher's opinion. But that, by her own opinion, was how Mrs. Shoder had decided to which section Ellie would go, which was the B Section. Now, back to the other side.

With Mrs. Shoder on her mind, as Ellie sat even more quietly, her thoughts drifted back to the first day of school, when she was twelve years old and beginning seventh grade...

Hey! Wait a minute! I have a good idea! We can drift back there with her! Are you okay with that? You are?! Great! Then let us be drifting.

It was the first day of the new school year and Ellie's first day in high school, well, Junior High School, but it was high school nonetheless, and she was super excited!

'Wait! Hold on, here,' you may be thinking. 'How could she be in high school if she was only twelve years old and in seventh grade?'

Well, I will tell you. It was a long time ago, remember, Ellie was a little girl—and a not-so-little girl—quite some time ago, so, as with almost everything else, schools were different then. Kindergarten was optional and kids who went to kindergarten only had to go for half of the day. Elementary School went from first through sixth grade. There was no such thing as Middle School. Junior High School included the seventh, eighth, and ninth grades. And Senior High School was tenth grade, eleventh grade, and twelfth grade. So, that is how Ellie, in seventh grade, could be in high school. Okay, now that you understand all of that, let us get back to her first day of high school.

It was Tuesday, September 7th, the day after both Labor Day and Ellie's 12th birthday. That made beginning high school, and going back to school after summer break, even more exciting to Ellie. To her, it felt like the best birthday present ever! Well, maybe not the 'best,' and maybe not 'ever,' but it was still doubly exciting! And because of that, Ellie had not slept too well the night before, but when did she ever sleep well?

Now, are you saying to yourself, 'Never!?' Because, if you are, you are right! But that night had been even worse than usual. She was so excited about starting high school that she hardly slept at all. However, you sure would not have known that if you had seen how energetically she skipped and trotted her way up Chestnut Street, across and down Third Avenue to Franklin Street, and up to the front of the high school, where she entered the building, 'bouncing' and 'dancing' uh… not literally, up the steps, through the doors and down the hallways, to her homeroom.

Uh! Third **Side Note:** Just in case you do not know what a homeroom is, I will explain that to you too. No, it was not where the teacher lived! Nor did the students live there! In fact, it was not a home at all; it was a classroom.

The homeroom was the classroom where the students went to begin and end each day. Every grade level was divided into just two groups because Ellie's school was small enough that no grade needed more than that. So, each grade had two homerooms, each with its own homeroom teacher.

At the start of the day, they met in their homeroom, so the homeroom teacher could take attendance, share any announcements that needed to be shared, and lead the kids in the reciting of the Pledge of Allegiance to The Flag, after which, one of the students offered the morning prayer. When all that was done, and the bell rang, the students were dismissed to go to their first class. Then, at the end of the day, after the last class was over, they all went back to their homeroom, where they received—if there were any—additional instructions and announcements before being dismissed to go home. Now that you understand all of that, let us go with Ellie, to her homeroom.

Ellie was one of the first students to enter Mr. Reems' classroom, which was her homeroom, so she was able to sit herself in the first seat of the row by the windows, right in front of the teacher's desk. That was her preferred seat in every classroom for two reasons. First, she liked being in the front row because, if she was not, she had a very difficult time seeing over or around whoever was sitting in front of her. Second, she loved being in the light that shone through the windows; it always made her feel... hmmm, how should I describe that feeling? Peaceful?

Comfortable? Happy? Yeah, all of those fit. She also liked looking at the clouds and playing the "imagination game," that is, seeing what images she could see in the clouds—like faces, houses, hands, horses—that was most definitely her favorite, ropes, glasses… well, you know, all kinds of things. Ellie had a very well-developed imagination, so she could always "see" things in the clouds, even if no one else could, and that was how she contented herself while everyone else was arriving and until the first bell rang.

After attendance was taken, the announcements were made, the Flag was Pledged to, the prayer was said, and the second bell rang, indicating that it was time to go to their first class, Mr. Reems dismissed everyone. As Ellie walked past him, who, by the way, was also her Math teacher, he said to her, "Now Ellie, make sure you do your best; you know you have to if you want to stay where you are."

"Oh, I will," Ellie replied, thinking he was just encouraging her. But that feeling faded away even before the day was over. Every one of her teachers, whether she had class with them that day or she just saw them in the hall and would have class with them on another day, said the same thing, not necessarily with the same words, but definitely with the same meaning.

As Ellie entered her Literature classroom, Mrs. O'Pelo said, in a tone that suggested she did not expect to see Ellie there, "Oh, Ellie, you are here. I think that is good, but just make sure you do what you need to do in order to stay here." Mrs. Refy, who was the teacher of the English class Ellie would be in, and who had been talking with Mrs. O'Pelo, reemphasized what Mrs. O'Pelo had said as she passed Ellie on her way out of the room.

In Health class, Mrs. Ro told her, "Make sure you work as hard as you can. I am sure you know that you must." And Mr. Lo Piado, her Social Studies teacher, told her she would need to work very hard, if she did not want to be removed from the A Section.

That was when Ellie realized why they were all saying what they were saying. She had known that Mrs. Shoder had recommended her to the B Section and that it was only because her dad had gone and talked to the principle that she had been reassigned to the A Section. What she had not known was that the reassignment was on a 'she-has-to-prove-herself' basis. It was Mrs. Lewdana, her Home Economics teacher and Mrs. Gowlind, her Music teacher, who explained to her, that if she wanted to be able to stay in the A Section, she had to get all As and Bs, nothing lower than that.

Well, apparently it had become pretty obvious by the time Ellie's afternoon classes began that she was feeling a bit deflated, because before she left her Science class, Mr. Caleses, after reminding her that she had to do excellent work in order to stay where she was, also told her that he was confident that she could do that. And, when Spanish class was over, Mr. Sens, the teacher of her Spanish class and who was also the father of one of the boys in Ellie's class, said to her, "Ellie, we all know that you know what you need to do to stay in the A Section, and that might not seem fair, especially since no one else has to do that. But Ellie, I know that you are a good student and a quick learner. I am certain that you can and will show everyone that the A Section is the right place for you to be."

Well, needless to say—but I will say it anyway— even though Mr. Caleses and Mr. Sens had helped Ellie feel a little better, she was still very sad and bothered. That was why, after school, when she got home, instead of going into the house, she climbed into their Catalpa tree, told the Angels all about her day and then, before climbing out of the tree, told the Angels, "I will show them! There is no way anyone is going to kick me out of the A Section! I know I can do it, and I will prove to them that I can, by doing it!"

And she did! In fact, she not only proved to everyone that she was a good learner and fit for the A Section, she was able to stay in the A Section that whole year, and the next year, and the next, and the ne… okay, I know that you have probably already figured out that that was where she stayed every year!!

But now, there she was again, sitting in her Catalpa tree, talking to the angels about how it seemed that she was going to have to prove herself again, but this time, it was not academically, it was sportingly.

'Huh?' you may be saying to yourself. 'Sportingly?'

Well, wonder not; I will explain. When Ellie was fourteen and began ninth grade, she decided to play sports. Now, that was a rather unexpected decision coming from Ellie because Ellie was not really what you would call a competitive person. She did like to play games and sports of almost all kinds, but she was never out to "beat" anyone. Ellie's goal was always to do the best that she could possibly do. Her aim was to do better today than she had done yesterday and do better tomorrow than she had done today. But she never wanted to just beat the other person or team. Ellie never wanted to do anything that would make anyone feel bad in any way for any reason. That was why the only person she ever 'competed' with—if you can call it that—was herself! She always worked hard to learn more, be able to do more, and to grow more.

Uh, explanation here, that grow more does not mean in size. When Ellie stopped growing, at twelve years old, she was only four feet ten inches tall. Well, maybe I should say she was four feet ten inches small! That was what everyone else said, and that was why everyone called her a Shrimp, a Dwarf, Tiny, Peanut... well, you get the idea.

Anyway, while Ellie was actually pretty good at most games and sports, no one ever believed that was possible, unless and until they saw it for themselves. But it also seemed that no one ever let what they saw in one game or sport carry over to any other game or sport.

"It does not make sense," Ellie sadly told the angels. "They did the same thing when I started hockey back in September. But I showed them that I could do it. So why are they doing this again with basketball?"

While the top branches swayed gently, Ellie sat quietly, as if listening to the angels, and at the same time, thought about her hockey experiences.

She remembered how hard it had been for her to run the four laps—one mile—around the track at the beginning of each practice. She never had been, still was not, and probably never would be able to run like others do because she had some problems with her ankles. Still, while it took her longer, because she had to run slower, she always ran the full mile.

She thought about how difficult it had been for her to reach the goal; she usually lost the ball to the other team before she even got halfway down the field. Still, even though she did not often score goals, she did a pretty good job at getting the ball away from the other team's players and passing it to one of her teammates, who did get it to the goal.

She also recalled how, after it was rather obvious that she could not effectively play the goalie, the other team always scored when she was the goalie, the coach took her out of play and assigned her to be the assistant manager. At first that made her quite sad, sad, really sa... well, I think you know how sad she was; it seemed to her to be just another indication that no one, even the coach, wanted her on the team. But! As the assistant coach, she had done a rather good job at suggesting moves and counter-moves. In fact, she had done well enough that the coach let her do all the coaching in a few of the games. And! Those games were games that her team won!

Hmmmm, Ellie thought, *maybe I could not play the game as well as the others, but I could coach the game.* As she sat quietly, looking up at the swaying branches, Ellie felt a calm, peaceful feeling coming over her. She felt sure that the Angels were letting her know that she did just fine because the one thing she never did was give up! And with that, as Ellie climbed down out of their Catalpa tree, got her school bag out of the wagon, and headed for the house, she resolved to move forward with basketball.

And so, she did!

At every practice and every game, Ellie did the best that she could do, which really was not too bad. Even though she rarely ever could get the ball into the hoop, she was quite good at keeping the ball when she had it. She was also very good at snatching the ball from the opposing team and passing it to one of her team members. That, of course, made the opposing team players mad. Soooooo…

It was one of the last games of the season, not the very last one, but one of the last. The game had been going quite well for Ellie's team, and one of the reasons it was going as well as it was going was because Ellie was doing a fantastic job of getting the ball from the other team's players and passing it to her team's player, who then took it to the hoop. Well, that made the other team's players rather mad, especially one girl in particular.

She was quite a tall young lady, a giant compared to Ellie, or so Ellie thought, and every time she got the ball, the ball went in the hoop. So, Ellie came up with a plan. Every time the 'giant' got the ball, Ellie scuttled in, took the ball, and dribbled it to the teammate closest to her, who then took the ball to their hoop.

Well, it was a good plan, and it was working quite well, so well, that the 'giant' got really mad, mad enough to decide to get rid of Ellie! Ergo, the next time she had the ball, she dribbled down the side of the court in front of the bleachers. Of course, Ellie ran to her, snatched the ball and tossed it to her closest teammate. That was when the 'giant' grabbed Ellie by the arm, swung her around, and threw her into the bleachers. Yes, you read that right—INTO the bleachers. Needless to say, but I will say it anyway, that hurt!

The referees stopped the game, all of Ellie's teammates and her coach ran to help her as she pulled herself out from between the bleacher seats. All her teammates and their coach asked her a trazillion times if she was okay. She told them she was mostly okay, except that she hurt quite a bit, but she insisted on finishing the game. With some hesitation, but because the 'giant' had been pulled out of the game, her coach did let her continue.

When the game ended, Ellie wasted no time leaving the gym, grabbing her stuff from the locker room, and hustling home. Well, perhaps I should say she hustled to their Catalpa tree because, before she went into the house, she climbed up to that big branch in the middle of the tree, sat down, leaned against the trunk, and looked up at the swaying branches where, she was certain, the Angels were waiting for her.

'I know I am not as good a player as all the other girls, but I thought I was at least doing okay,' Ellie silently told the angels. 'But now my coach thinks I probably should not play basketball. I guess I... well, I just... oh, I do not know! Is there really anything I can do?'

Ellie sat quietly, listening to the breeze blow through the tree. She watched the birds perch on Catalpa's branches. She looked up at the highest branches and watched them sway. And as she did, she heard again what she was certain the Angels were saying to her, "Ellie, you did just fine because the one thing you did not do is the one thing you never do, and that is give up!"

As Ellie thought about those words, she realized, perhaps for the first time, perhaps not, but most definitely in a way and to a degree that she had never realized before. God does not compare us to others. He does not measure us by anyone else's successes or failures. He just expects us to do our best in all that we do, and continue to learn, grow, and progress to the best of our own abilities.

With a calm feeling of renewed self-worth, Ellie climbed down to the ground and headed for the house. So many times, in relation to so many things, Ellie had found herself, saying to herself, **"I had to prove myself."** But now, it was so comforting to realize—to actually know—that we do not have to prove ourselves to anyone! It is what God thinks of us that is important, and He really does love us and expects no more from us than the best that we can do, the best that we can be, and the best that we can become!

ABOUT THE AUTHOR

Eileen DiStasio-Clark is the second oldest of four children. She is the mother of eleven children and grandmother to twenty-three grandchildren, to date. As a member of The Church of Jesus Christ of Latter-Day Saints, she serves in various positions, teaching, leading, and ministering to children, youth, and adults. Currently, she is also a Family History Missionary. Eileen established the Pursuit of Excellence Institute of Family Education, a non-profit organization focused on strengthening the family. Presently she holds an A.A., a B.A., and an M.A. in Clinical Psychology and is working on the completion of her Doctoral Degree.